NINE DUTCH POETS

NINE DUTCH POETS

◆◆◆◆◆◆◆

Pocket Poets Series No. 42

**City Lights Books
San Francisco**

Cover photo by Maya Pejić

Library of Congress Card No. 82-4224
ISBN: 0-87286-135-X

Distributed in the Netherlands, Flanders, Scandinavia,
and Germany by IN DE KNIPSCHEER B.V. (Ltd.)
                    Schouwtjeslaan 23b
                    Haarlem, Holland

CITY LIGHTS BOOKS are edited by Lawrence Ferlinghetti &
Nancy J. Peters and published at the City Lights Bookstore,
261 Columbus Avenue, San Francisco, USA 94133.

FOREWORD

Since 1978, Amsterdam's One World Poetry Foundation has been bringing poets to the Netherlands from around the world, with many thousands attending the annual festivals. At last year's "War Against War" festival, the idea for this book took shape when One World Poetry director Benn Posset raised the possibility of an anthology of Dutch poets who would be touring the U.S. in the Spring of 1982.

The poets included herein have been associated either with the experimentalists after World War II (called the Fifti-ers), with the COBRA group of artists (COpenhagen-BRussels-Amsterdam), and/or are generally sympathetic to the One World Poetry movement toward peace symbolized by "Hollanditis." (A statement on it by the venerable and respected Dutch humanist, Anton Constandse, is also included.) Two of the poets are also major Dutch painters.

As a part of the celebration of 200 years of peaceful Dutch-American relations, most of these poets will be touring U.S. cities (including New York, Chicago, Ann Arbor, Boulder, and San Francisco) this Spring, spreading their own very inde-pendent kind of diverse beauty, and also hopefully spreading that very communicable virus, Hollanditis.

Scott Rollins & Lawrence Ferlinghetti
February 1982

ACKNOWLEDGMENTS

This book has been published with the financial and editorial assistance of the foundation for the Promotion of the Translation of Dutch Literary Works. Scott Rollins was the editor in charge of translation in Amsterdam.

Thanks are due also to the editors and publishers of books and magazines in which some of the translations in this volume previously appeared. For Lucebert: *Modern Poetry in Translation 27-28* (© Modern Poetry in Translation, Ltd., London, 1976); *Writing in Holland and Flanders 32*, (Amsterdam, 1973); *Poetry Review* Vol. 64 No. 4 (© The Poetry Society, London 1974); *Dremples 2* Winter 1975, Amsterdam; *DAM Poetry International Documents*, Vol. 1 No. 2 Summer 1981, Rotterdam. For Remco Campert: *Writing in Holland and Flanders 35*, Amsterdam, 1978; *Modern Poetry in Translation 27-28*; *Delta* Vol. 6 No. 1 (© Delta International Publication Foundation, Amsterdam, 1963). For Judith Herzberg: *Modern Poetry in Translation 27-28*; Wilfion Books—a poem from *Quartet: An Anthology of Dutch & Flemish Poetry*, Paisley, Scotland, 1978. For J. Bernlef: *Trends: The Paisley College of Technology Literary Magazine*, Paisley, Scotland, Vol. 2 No. 4, 1979; *Contemporary Literature in Translation*, final issue, Vancouver, B.C.; *Cross-Cultural Review 2 'Five Dutch Poets'*, Merrick, N.Y., 1979.

CONTENTS

Karel Appel

◆◆◆

KAREL APPEL was born April 25, 1921, in Amsterdam. He is considered one of the major modern Dutch painters and was a part of the COBRA movement. He lived 33 years in Paris and has now passed 25 years in New York. He has just had his first book of poems published in Paris, most written during the last three years (although "Mad Talk" dates from 1947). He wrote the poems in Dutch, French, and English.

Poetry:

Océan Blessé (Wounded Ocean): Poems and Drawings, Éditions Galilée, Paris, 1982.

AMSTERDAM

City of the east and the west
I always see you in my memories
city of bazaars and ships
and harbors and oceans, city of cranes
and pubs, of canals and smells
laid out low behind the wild
dunes of the sea.

Hardly rising above the wild waves,
you lie low under the dark heavy sky,
gorged with water, sunk low in the sky
as though held by invisible hands
safe from the engulfing storms
that come over you like some fierce lover.

City of my youth, low and lower than
the sea, girt by its roaring
love for you, old town of my dreams,
white with snow, where I lived on an old canal
with my very first love
narrow streets full of light, full of music
alleys where the beautiful girls
gave their passion like fans
turning in the perfumes of the evening breeze—
magical northern city of
islands, conditioned by sea and sky
mysterious city
the old neighborhood where I lived

ALL KINDSA WAYS

Life? I'll tell you
life is a lightbulb
that one day slips out of your hands

and the horizon of the future
is like a jelly-fish on the move

nobody knows how far it is
between life and death
mind and spirit
thinking and feeling
nobody knows

you don't mind any more
if you don't have the sky in your pocket
like a windmill full of summer days

the great thing would be to
just walk away from this planet of ours
up into the sky of love
with a gaudy parrot on your head

as for the skyscrapers
all they want is to see us
standing in the city streets
and staring like bewildered monkeys

I don't care
you don't care
we don't care

FUNNY STORY, A KIND OF DREAM

For the good heads
and the bad heads
an image in red
an image in pink

something else goes by
at the speed of light
a stone bird, a metal hand
a black mirror

what's that two-headed donkey doing
jumping over my head?

an ant makes a getaway on a bike
pedalling like mad
your body's on fire

NAKED DREAMS

Earthquake everywhere
and naked disaster
prowling around
between night and day

the air still
no wind, no sound
I'm not there
she's not there

time naked as air
as the sky, as water
as myself

her breast was always
like the curved wave
falling on the beach

SENTIMENTAL SAXOPHONE

Your old saxophone heart
is flying, full of melodies
over the nostalgic mountains

your lips
like white apples
are asking for pleasure

panic and unhappiness
lie low
in the maelstrom of your mind

getting home and seeing
the faces of the stars
change the landscape into
a huge lumbering crocodile

way up on the yellow hills
the saxophone plays
the sounds of a sentimental ocean
and the tide goes out

birds fly by crying
and their tears
turn into clouds

tired hunting up the past
the tourist is now asking around
for the prophet with the golden pig

COPENHAGEN HARBOR

The master has spoken
animal head, huge eye
staring you in the face

fight the sun
drink the rain
the sea's gone berserk

Wotan talking

when the giant
wags his tongue
the boats go
up and down
up and down
up and down

the mountains look on
with a thousand eyes
drowned in aqua vitae

THE FORGOTTEN ANGELS

We feel nothing
only the light growing
we feel that life
has forgotten her wings

the world has gone
from sleepy space
to a technological penitentiary
with the sound-tape of human rights
babbling on through the night

one smile, one angel smile
might burn the shadows on the roof
and let us see the stars
like flowers

WOUNDED OCEAN

Wounded water
deep wailing water
deep red water

the ocean is wounded
like an iceberg
running with blood

the ocean is wounded
the ocean is wounded

the voice of the ocean
will never come back
never
come back

who killed the whale?

A DONKEY'S DESIRE

Whoever you are
go in and kiss
kiss and kiss and kiss

without looking
without asking
without knowing

let your eyes
make a world
of each image

make it with anybody

not always the same people
not lovers, not thinkers, not strangers

forget the categories

the red, the grey, the green
the blue, the black
the fat elephants and the thin snakes

give life a change

All these poems written in English

MAD TALK

Mad is mad
madmen are mad
to be mad is everything
to be everything is mad
not to be mad is everything
to be everything is not mad
to be nothing is to be mad
to be mad is nothing
everything is mad
mad is everything
because everything is mad
yet everything is mad
and not to be mad is to be mad
nothing is mad after all
non-madmen are mad
madmen are not mad
mad is mad
mad mad mad

J. Bernlef

◆◆◆

J. BERNLEF is the pen name of Henk Marsman. He was born in the village of Saint-Pancras on 14 January, 1937, but moved to Amsterdam shortly thereafter, and has been living there ever since. Bernlef is one of Holland's most prolific authors, having written some fifty books since his first publication in 1960. Besides fourteen volumes of poetry he has written novels, plays, essays on modern poetry, jazz, modern classical music and numerous short stories. He is an amateur jazz pianist and has translated much American poetry into Dutch, including Marianne Moore, William Carlos Williams, and Elizabeth Bishop. Besides writing numerous articles he now is busy with a long study of the work of the American painter, Edward Hopper.

Poetry:

Kokkels (Cockles), 1960
Morene, 1961
Dit verheugd verval (This Happy Ruin), 1963
Ben even weg (Just Stepped Out For a Minute), 1965
De schoenen van de dirigent (The Conductor's Shoes), 1966
Bermtoerisme (Roadside Picnicking), 1968
Het testament van een Vliegende Hollander (The Flying Dutchman's Testament), 1969
Hoe wit kijkt een eskimo (How White Does An Eskimo Look), 1970
Grensgeval (On the Border), 1972
Brits (Cot), 1975
Zwijgende man (Silent Man), 1976
Gedichten 1960-1970 (Poems), 1977
Stilleven (Still Life), 1979
De Kunst van het verliezen (The Art of Losing), 1980

Novels:

Sneeuw (Snow), 1973
Meeuwen (Seagulls), 1975
De man in het midden (The Man in the Middle), 1976
Onder ijsbergen (Under Icebergs), 1981

ON THE DEATH
OF ROBERT LOWELL

Once again you're in the dark hall
your back against the wall and your
face towards the screen, once again
you're imprisoned in the dead corner.

Here they come, from the left,
running and grabbing at furniture
shrieking children on their backs, screaming
they fly across the bending bridge.

But even if water would burn
I'd still be sitting here at the side
figuring that they're dead now or too old
or half forgotten and besides
run so many times and worn, I

Rocket out of my chair
because some dainty Oxford English voice
announces that what I'm witnessing here
happened on the exact day I was first
born laid in a cradle and baptized Henk.

When time evaporates into image
all comparisons fail: the child
is drawn from under the ruins
crumpled in its clothes, the woman
weeps soundlessly against a shop front
(advertising *rebaja*, sales), the lieutenant

takes it in his arms and says: Is this,
is this maybe your child?

Picture of dumb grief
(even the blood the voice calls for
afterwards has been shed long ago)
I can't help but get up
and leave the movie theater.

Back home the radio announces
Robert Lowell, poet,
died in New York
at the age of only sixty.

When image evaporates into time
all comparisons fail and when
water keeps burning on the screen
when the dead corner gets flooded
with more and more blood
which is forgiven him now
in exchange for some poems
and his life.

Translated by Peter Nijmeijer
from: *De kunst van het verliezen*

THE JAILER'S LAUGHTER

Each wall is a door
the prisoner dreams

Each door is a wall
the philosopher posits

Between the two
the jailer floats

Inaudible
no one can see him

Walking in and out
with two keys

One for the prisoner
one for the philosopher

Eye to eye
a comical sight

Two beards smoothly
fitting together

Translated by Peter Nijmeijer
from: *De kunst van het verliezen*

UNCLE CARL: A HOME MOVIE

Saw a home movie today. Uncle Carl
caught unawares in a small boat near the lakes.
Three weeks later he was dead, no longer susceptible to
    celluloid.

How good it would be to have a movie of his dying
the projectionist, reeling off his last breath
in slow motion the fogging of his eyes the falling of that
hand along the iron bedstead, showing it again and again.

Or at topspeed, so that Uncle Carl's dying
would take on something merry, a rollicking dance on a
    creaking bed
the embrace of an invisible woman

who kisses him awake on the rewind; the eyes
again turn their gaze, looking into the lens, the hand pointing.
Uncle Carl is alive, Uncle Carl is dead.

Translated by Scott Rollins
from: *Gedichten 1960-1970*

ERIK SATIE

Like a sledge through snow
like a wiggling little finger
like a storm in a forgotten red label
teacup
3 times 'like' and still haven't said
who Satie is
who was too young
for this world of old hat.

I put on his *Sports et Divertissements*
20 demonstrations of daintiness
and write
like an elderly lady in a playground
like birds' toes in fresh earth
like dooh like dah
my daughter screams
and yah
c'est ça
c'est Satie.

Translated by Theo Hermans
from: *Bermtoerisme*

PAIN

Sometimes a stone will
grow within the body
nesting there festering
like a red-hot lava

With the pain
the world withdraws from
my sight

(In the stone's
heart there lives
an eye that is
never seen)

Once liberated
I pass it around
as evidence: that's
what my pain looked like

(In the stone's
heart there lives
a memory that is
never remembered)

Translated by Theo Hermans
from: *Zwijgende man*

SILENT MAN

He who wants to say something
needs winter
bare leafless boughs

Trace of birds not
their whistling water
inaccessibly hard and smooth

He who wants that
has saved something
in his eyes
that is called watching

He who can do that
knows what he says
best preserved
in his silence

Translated by Theo Hermans
from: *Zwijgende man*

OBSERVER

where there's nothing to see
the observer focuses
on differences

and language shapes
the inner
landscape

he arranges the mountains
in a sentence made
of words

conjugates the snow shower
in its flakes
his foot inflects the ice

with neither conclusions
nor compass
he arrives home

Translated by Theo Hermans
from: *Hoe wit kijkt een eskimo*

Remco Campert

♦♦♦

REMCO CAMPERT was born in The Hague, 28 July, 1929. He was a part of the Dutch "Fiftiers" movement. In 1976 Campert was awarded the Dutch State Prize for his entire oeuvre of poetry (The P.C. Hooft Prize). All his works display a resentment of pomposity and profundity. This leads him to wrap the serious, angry nucleus of his work in easily digestible, light-footed language. He couples a talent for registering even the most minute changes in society with an obstinate integrity, a refusal to be led astray by any illusion.

Poetry:

Vogels vliegen toch (And Yet Birds Fly), 1951
Een standbeeld opwinden (Winding Up a Statue), 1952
Berchtesgaden , 1953
Het huis waarin ik woonde (The House I Lived In), 1955
Met man en muis (Lost With All Hands), 1955
Bij hoog en bij laag (Whether You Like It Or Not), 1959
Dit gebeurde overal (This Happened Everywhere), 1962
Hoera, hoera (Hurrah, Hurrah), 1965
Mijn leven's liederen (The Songs of My Life), 1968
Betere tijden (Better Times), 1970
Alle bundels gedichten (The Campert Poetry), 1976

In Translation:

No Holds Barred, translated by John Scott, Rupert Hart-Davis, London, 1965 & Mayflower paperback, London, 1968.
Gangster Girl, translated by John Scott, Rupert Hart-Davis, London, 1968.
In The Year of the Strike: Selected Poems, Poetry Europe Series, Rapp & Whitling, London, 1968.
Included in *Living Space: Poems of the Dutch Fiftiers*, edited by Peter Glassgold, New Directions, New York, 1979.

CREDO

I believe in a river
flowing from the ocean to the mountains
I ask no more of poetry
than to chart this river

I don't want to bring forth water from rocks
but I want to carry water to rocks
dry black rock
becoming blue water rock

but the newspapers want something else
the headlines to be dry and black
to throw up dams and demand
diversion

Translated by Greta Kilburn

POETRY IS AN ACT

Poetry is an act
of affirmation. I affirm
that I'm alive, that I do not live alone.

Poetry is a future, thinking
of the following week, of another country,
of you, when you are old.

Poetry is my breath, moving
my feet, hesitantly sometimes
over the earth that asks me to.

Voltaire had smallpox, but
cured himself by drinking lots including
200 pints of lemonade: that is poetry.

Or take the surf. Breaking
on the rocks but not ever broken
and rising and therein being poetry.

Each word that is written
is an attack upon old age.
After all, death wins, you can be sure,

but death is merely the silence in the hall
after the last word has been spoken

Death is a moving emotion.

Translated by Greta Kilburn

1975

Funny years, these years,
nothing comical, lots of flops
rolling stones without moss.

Poetry, crippled, goes back home
the warm lamp
the small pain of crying mommy-daddy
grief about the bygone birthday
once more nature consoles
once more that wretched God turns up
now disguised as a neo-conservative student
or a neo-marxist nitwit.

But we too
when we had a shot at the sublime
had nothing to offer anyone
that provided a place for safety
food in a stomach
shears to cut through barbed wire
hardly a rag for the bleeding
or beauty that burns a poem.

Dishevelled in snow-covered plains
deserts caught in walls
the camps cellars and cages
where a man becomes the inhuman other.

All those dreams all those years
time and again the child at the burnt down station

the high-pitched shrieking in the barracks
where your voice, that lovely vase,
was kicked to bits.

And outside the gates
the cold cameraman
always worried about his material.

Writing, that silly luxury
where breathing is already an extravagance
and eating everything on your plate.

The best talents spent on liquor,
on renown, on vanity,
on heroin
or in the asylum,
with a position on a committee
or jumping from a window
or frightened under the wife's skirts
or losing oneself in analyses:
napalm of words
across the skin of the language.

Ah,
slap us in the face
so that we wake up
so that our emotion does not
lose itself in small bleating
so that we pick up our beds again
and go wandering with the beggar boy
with the beggar girl.

Translated by Greta Kilburn

THIS HAPPENED EVERYWHERE

This happened everywhere:
the jobless loafers,
the wounded veterans dreaming
of a corporate street,
the restless retired old men
who had suffered great injustice.

The damps of the night
still hung in the city—
tired and shivering I left the barroom,
the morning grew up the mountains.

A blind man was selling lottery tickets
to stray dogs and limping alcoholics
and in front of an embassy
a buxom maid stood scrubbing the stoop.
But unless you're lying with a whore or your wife,
cities are sexless in the morning.

And the crazy posters
for the bullfight the soccer game
the hundredth show—
letters letters letters
the circus left long ago.

I went on
into the healthy countryside
over the chalk-white roads,
while the thirsty sun drank me dry—

or took the tram,
my ticket wet with the first rain,
back to my furnished room,
the unpaid rent and a senseless sleep.

Translated by Ramon du Pré

POEM

And if we love, have love
among much paper, hollow men and metal,
then let us love as I see fit:

To love with the quiet of disquiet, not
that of routine, to lose each other's eyes
and rediscover them, to pass by houses

into the countryside, caressed by unfamiliar
vines, taste the wind on tongues of every kind,
see the moon and the sun in a chartless path.

And let friends age quickly, becoming
cherished legends, and that plot of earth
fruitful only where we tread.

Translated by Greta Kilburn

THEATER

I take you
backstage
where the actors pinch ass
play cards
read stock market quotes
stare at the dust
do yoga
cough behind their hands

Where they're between two lives
do not fulfill a single role
and yet are in their place.

On that spot
between coming on and taking off the makeup
between stomping and showering
we too belong.

Bodies about to budge
mouths open to speak
but not yet . . .

Translated by Scott Rollins

A BIT OF NATURE

A bit of nature
at times I'm all in favor
a tuft of grass between the stone steps
or a swishing elder tree

Tiny ladybugs
small prickling on your arm
beaches full one time
when you were fond of me

In the backyard
the magnolia is in bloom
and I'm getting much better
with the indoor plants

But raped by Tarzan
naked in a jungle
that of all things
is what you'll dream

Translated by Greta Kilburn

Jules Deelder

◆◆◆

JULES DEELDER was born in Rotterdam, 24 November, 1944. He calls his work Neon-Realism and Neon-Romanticism. Deelder began publishing in the late sixties and is unique on the Dutch scene. His absurd often black humoristic texts are machine-gunned at his audience. His readings are genuine performances; his deadpan antics pare modern city life to the bone.

Poetry:

Gloria Satoria , 1969
Dag en nacht geopend (Open Day and Night), 1970
Boe! (Boo!), 1972
Op de deur knop na (Everything but the Kitchen Sink), 1972
De zwarte jager (The Black Hunter), 1973
Moderne gedichten (Modern Poems), 1979
Sturm und Drang, 1980

Prose:

Proza, 1976

AGRARIAN RHAPSODY

Heard the first
blackbird sing
Found the first
wild violet
Chestnuts in
blossom

Seen the first
dutchman's breeches
Observed the first
swallow
First meal without
lights

Found flowering
coltsfoot
Heard the first
cuckoo
Cut the first
grass

Cherries in
blossom
Pears in bloom
Appleblossomtime

Picked the first
strawberries
Currants ripe
Cherries ripe

Oats in the field
ripe
First pears
Last meal without
lights

First apples
First grapes
Last bath out in
the open
Swallows gone

Cut the last
grass
Stove lit for the
first time
First frost
Last rose

The first snow
falling

Translated by the author
from: *Dag en nacht geopend*

DER UNTERGANG DES ABENDLANDES

Stretched full-length
in skyblue bath
he absentmindedly
takes off his shades
to gaze thru those
he wears beneath
at the prehistoric
ostrich emerging some-
where near his feet
from clouds of steam

And as he slowly
evaporates into a gas
of unknown composition
from his crystal throat
still bursts the Mad
Queen's Air

—Look up my ass if
the teawater's boiling—

Next a multi-colored
lizard silently
issues from his navel

*Translated by the author
from: Gloria Satoria*

EXHIBITION

Here a stone and
over there some pink-
rimmed glasses and
further down the Key
to Kingdom Come
as well as 37 names
of people missing and
the measurements
of Liberace's Mom

Next to these a pool
that holds no water
a phone booth on an empty
windswept square
some suburb not yet sup-
plied with sidewalks
a rainbow and a mitre
and a chair

Followed by seven swans
swimming in the
moonlight
a lightbulb
lit without no plug
a box of ammo
left over from the '30s
and a dead fish
wrapped up in the *Times*

Translated by the author
from: Dag en nacht geopend

BIRDS OF PASSAGE

Many of those
that freed themselves
from the dazzling
streams of light

came in sharp contact
with the copper
dome of the tower
making it sound like a drum

and then fell like flashes
into the water below
followed slowly by
a cloud of feathers

resembling a shower of
golden flakes

Translated by the author

PYTHON PLACE

(part 4711)

In which the Queen finally flips and new doctor Nosy gets hurt real bad while buggering the queer mayor's Siamese twins as the jampacked Hospital is blown to bits by a gang of SS in full dress just flown in from Hollywood by zeppelin at the request of the local KKK—for jewish colored catholics only—as to advise in the construction of the new Public Baths on Prussic-acid Road where as it is 'Neverdead,' switched-on home for the agèd, goes up in flames at the hands of the schizofrantic renegade son of an apparently dead brother of some psychic aunt of the nymfo sister-in-law of the megalomaniac housekeeper of the Lone Ranger's, who at this time, aided by perpetual Pronto, is busily erecting in the schoolyard a small but nonetheless stylish scaffold on which shortly on occasion of the Plastic Anniversary of the Chamber of Commies Institute for the Advance of Virginal Anteaters are to be publicly emasculated with a pair of rusty gardenshears at the insistence of the editor of the local newspaper, *The Python Place Paranoia Post*, who, by the by, is about to be going to flatten himself and his chopper en route to the Big Deal Palace right on the corner of Librium Lane against a tree that should have been removed, according to the script, some three installments earlier by a dozen or so escaped and criminally insane, whereupon he commends his soul into the hands of Santa Claus, patrolling the banks of the River Speed, where the Annual Cosa Nostrean Fishing Contest for Unsanitary Oldtimers threatens to turn into massive slaughter as competitors go for each other with trepans and army surplus hypodermics singing 'The International' and other obscene hymns, cheered on by the Mixed Crematorial Choir with Sir Goddamn Urgent conducting and featuring Count Chuckle and his Cold Turkey Kickers, repeated atttempts at mediation by the Bank of No Returns branch manager notwithstanding, who is just about to bury alive for the entertainment of his beautifully embalmed wife the ghastly mutilated heirs to the legendary Marihuana Millions at the foot of Ye' Majestic Olde Oak Tree near the stagnant waterfall from which after some technicolor showtrial he's hung by his own suspenders upon confessing under heavy torture—administered by fifty boy scouts under the expert command of Scoutmaster Himmler—to having tampered with the books for at least the 123 years, his wife's remains meanwhile being assaulted without pause before his very eyes by all political parties till they finally fall apart into a thousand fragments to lay scattered at the feet of the Fool Board of Lunatics of the Pythonian Institute for the Study of Rustic Aberrations amongst the Mummified Parts of the Population, as it returns totally plastered in open carriages from the Perennial Convention of Slug Manufacturers at the nearby resort of Golgotham where now only a few thousand test cases remain riddled with bullets and bathing in blood to vainly plead for mercy to the Secretary of Fate who's far too busy anyhow cutting the dope in the neoncomic town hall of Python Place packed with scribes and pharisees as well as with the purpleclad members of the 'Attaboy Brass Band,' all 365 of them direct straightline descendants of that Grand Python, once the uncrowned king of Python Place and far surroundings; and all those present are filled with joy as during the last strains of 'Alexander's Ragtime Band' God-the-Very-Father, wrapped in the 'Star-spangled Banner,' comes descending by V2 from his Heavenly Abodes to Personally present the graduates from the School for Mutual Misunderstanding with their certificates—and lo! as if by miracle the waterfall stirs into motion and they all lived heavily ever after . . . .

Translated by the author
from: *Dag en nacht geopend*

TRIPLE EXPOSURE

(At home)

He managed again to get up before noon today
He reads his paper and drinks his tea
He's humming

In Bavaria some 63-year-old farmer's wife
and her 30-year-old son
for fear of being bewitched hung themselves
in the barn before the eyes of the farmer
aged 60

He folds the paper shut and puts it down on
top of those from the preceding days
from which he can recall—among others—
a Canadian girl dead at the age of 9
tho looks like she were 90

He turns on the radio and gets filled in on
liverwurst

(On the road)

He waits for the streetcar in a shelter with
a pair of scales
He weighs nine stone, clothes included

Behind one of the windows across the street
someone who's been ill for years lies still
on a high white bed

The conductor tries to talk him into buying
a diary for the benefit of some retreat
for strained streetcar drivers

He observes a man who gets off at each stop
gets back on and pays again and again

(On the scene)

He drinks beer in a bar where the clock stands
fixed at ten to three for all of 30 years
He swaps some information

Like no he wouldn't know where to score for a
blow and in exchange
he gets to hear of Danny's dose
New films are briefly spoken of

He makes a friend pick up his check
pretends he's out of cigarettes and after a
short conference ends up with 15 white pills

Then he splits and seems hardly surprised to
find he leaves no prints in the recent snow

Translated by the author

Judith Herzberg

♦♦♦

JUDITH HERZBERG was born in Amsterdam on 4 November, 1934. Since her first volume of poetry in 1963 she has written scripts for TV, film and plays for the theater. She was a staff member of the Institute for Research of Dutch Theater from 1972-1973. A selection of her poetry was included in a 1974 anthology of women poets from Holland and Flanders, edited and translated by Manfred Wolf, for Two Windows Press in Berkeley. She recently wrote the screenplay for the film *Charlotte*, about the life of the German Jewish painter Charlotte Salomon.

Poetry:

Zeepost (Slow Boat), 1963
Beemdgras (Meadow Grass), 1968
Vliegen (Flies), 1970
Strijklicht (Grazing Light), 1971
27 Liefdesliedjes (27 Love Songs), 1971
Botshol, 1980

Plays:

Dat het's octhends ochtend wordt (So Mornings Become Morning/De deur stond open (The Door Stood Open), 1974

Diaries:

Het maken van gedichten (Making Poems), 1977
Charlotte, dagboek bij een film (Charlotte, diary of a film), 1980

1944

Be glad you're still alive—
and was, and was, but sang
my body lies over the ocean.

And looked up the birds
in their trembling summer.
Crossbills, orioles
were still around
and kingfishers over the ditch.

Radar-jamming silver foil threads
brilliantly woven through their nests.

A joyful summer, full
of green promise, they flew
anywhere and back again
wherever they wanted in their peace
gulls even over the sea.

Translated by Shirley Kaufman

1945

We were having heroes to tea
they sat together on the sofa
they had absolutely no
conversation, I stared and stared
'til they turned shy
they had no way of coping
with such peace.

Translated by Shirley Kaufman

BAD ZWISCHENAHN, 1964

The bride hobbles out of church on too high heels
and laughs her shrill laugh under topheavy hair
and lets herself be kissed by the uncles and stands
between the graves and looks her small new husband in the
    eyes.

Begonias burst into bloom, ivy grows
over the medieval churchfront, all for the photographer.
Now the pastor can explain
the old altar-piece to us.
The man beating Jesus must keep roaming;
he is the Jewish people, the Wandering Jew,
last seen, according to legend, in Bremen, 1510.

I swallow and ask him in this warm and stifling Germany
why his church honors the heroes of the First War,
not those of the Second, with a plaque.
Answering himself, me, god, the photographer, the dead,
He says: It is no longer easy for any of us
to be who we are and still go on.

Translated by Shirley Kaufman

WE LIVE

We live on the heritage of our will.
Not one cell or tastebud is still the same
in this our present year
as in that short past our beginning.

We equal forty-two generations of mice
or perhaps more. Probably more.
They live fast and small. Not one
of fourteen years ago is moving still.

And yet, even these great-
great-grandchildren
of our primal feelings and intentions—
they got the message.

They rustle behind dry wall paper
and scamper across the floor.

Translated by Manfred Wolf

WHITE LETTERS

Whoever painted *Black Panther*
in white letters on the church at night
is not subject to doubt.

Neither is the man who comes to wipe it off
by day, an Indonesian who works for the city;
he does it for a living, just a job.

Still, as efforts go, both seem strange.
I know something they'd be better off doing,
but on the scales of my conscience
bullets of need and loaves of lead
always weigh against each other.

Translated by Manfred Wolf

MAGIC

Before the war all that was different—
boxes full of pointed Caran d'Ache
in all the colors of the rainbow
but if you slid them open
everything changed because
before the war there was a war at hand.

Look how sweet children
look how sweet we were
we locked our mother into the cellar
we blew up frogs with a straw.

And when we slid those boxes open
fireworks jumped out on parachutes
that were shot down at once
and, falling, striped the sky.

So it was all
our own fault
as she often used to say.

Translated by the author

VOCATION

And when they asked her what she wanted to be
she said 'Invalid' and saw herself,
legs motionless in brownish plaids,
pushed by devoted husband and pale sons;
not even a stamp to paste herself,
not a letter to write, no trip to take.
Then she would be really free at last,
look as sad as she pleased, take her
turn before other in stores, be up
in front at parades, no pretty clothes,
and every night sobbing softly
she would say,'Not on account of myself
but all that trouble for you.'
And both boys would always
stay with her, devote
their lives to her, and nothing
would ever happen to her
never, never would she wear out.

Translated by Manfred Wolf

OLD AGE

Later, when I am feeble-minded
with lapdog and frightskin
I'll keep a bottle warm
against me and talk
to you in my sleep.
If you can understand now
what I'm going to mean then
crackling withered stem that I'll be
I will not feel so broken off
more like a blown-out dandelion.
You hear me babble?
There go my little parachutes.

Translated by the author

Lucebert

◆◆◆

LUCEBERT is the pen name of L.J. Swaanswijk, born September 15, 1924, in Amsterdam. Lucebert is a poet-painter whose great output of poetry in the 1950s resulted in his being awarded the Dutch State Prize for Literature in 1967. He has since concentrated mainly on his painting. The name Lucebert means "luce" = light, and "bert" is a transliteration of "brecht" which means bright. Lucebert is the son of a furniture maker who grew up in Amsterdam before the Second World War. He was sent to a work camp in Germany during the war. After having traveled a great deal he settled in Bergen (North Holland) in 1953. He took part in the Fiftiers movement in the Netherlands and is considered its most eloquent spokesman.

Poetry:

Triangel in de jungle (Triangle in the Jungle), 1951
De dieren der democratie (The Beasts of Democracy), 1951
Apocrief (Apocryphal), 1952
De analfabetische naam (The Illiterate Name), 1952
De Amsterdamse school (The Amsterdam School), 1952
Van de afgrond en de luchtmens (Of the Abyss and the Airman), 1953
Alfabel (Alfabell), 1955
Amulet (Amulet), 1957
Val voor vliegengod (Trap for the Lord of the Flies), 1959
Gedichten 1948-1963 (Poems), 1965
... en morgen de hele wereld (... and tomorrow the world), 1972
Verzamelde gedichten 1949-1974 (Collected Poems), 1974
Dames en heren (Ladies & Gentlemen) (with Bert Schierbeek), 1976
Oogsten in de dwaaltuin (Reaping in the Labyrinth), 1981

In Translation:

Included in *Four Dutch Poets*, translated by Peter Nijmeijer, Transgravity Press, London, 1976.
Included in *Living Space, Poems of the Dutch Fiftiers*, edited by Peter Glassgold, New Directions, New York, 1979.

BREYTEN BREYTENBACH MAY LOOK AT THE MOON

1

The faceless swine snorted from afar
and today the report arrived here
that after two years in the cold stone jug
you were given a thin mattress and a slice of moon

This poem shames itself by being a poem
rage wants weapons other than words
yes it shames itself by being a poem and not a shot
that—poet—could kill your executioner

2

Under a shower of blows
they turned your body
into a shrunken raincoat
and to throw that down somewhere
after many showers you got a mattress
oh—their methods are becoming so refined
now they even serve a piece of moon
like a crust of bread a slovenly mother
flings to her scrawny brood
but they're still waiting for the best
that in gratitude you'll write an ode
to the thugs who want to kill you slowly

3

Pain has no number
there will be days like years
and minutes that trot
like an ocean without a horizon

Seconds seem piles of small lips
that briefly may swallow the blade of the moon
and memories are inflamed glasses
like shards of fire on the nose of darkness

Old sore—poet—you can see it fester
when even newborn guitars start throwing up
under the cant of evangelizing hands
swindle—poet—you've so often seen through

You've so often seen in a far distant past
a pale spirit declare itself god
dissatisfied with his boorish mouldering
he then called himself good and god of the whites

Translated by Anthony Akerman & Peter Nijmeijer

SMALL STRATEGIST

The small solar table was immense
where as a child I played my dreams
the mountains here the valleys there
and the danger in between with its wild beard

Back then everything was yellow under happy eyes
not a shadow was mapped out
even the despot remained unweighed and in silence
played off against the slaves forever singing

Translated by Scott Rollins
from: *Oogsten in de dwaaltuin*

NIGHT WORK

Staring so hard at the shards I
am so glad I'm still in one piece
the house full of strangers guests
coughing all night long before my mirrors
how can it be that the deceit of their day
can go on so rebellious in their night
has an angular world been invented
that they have to round off with difficulty

And the greatest of all ghosts a shirker sweats
sneezes the air that despises him
the sucked-in gut of his prim mouth
is a cheek lived in by a trembling child
his once clear speech when parsed falls apart
into a garbage dump of cries and groaning
and all he points to with threadthin gestures
are watering places true but only for the unapproachable

Translated by Scott Rollins
from: *Oogsten in de dwaaltuin*

THE INDIGO EATER

Clouds like wolves above the roasted mountains
and in my dark room the table sagging
with the grapes in the valley with the crocks
full of tardy tears and on the horizon
socialism fades: meager fruit of often fasting

All I have to do is just walk to the open window
a diamond mouth breathed upon by the moon
to be sure to get sleepless hands from the power
to demolish masks in attics and the jubilant
tremolo of overproduction: the fatal fountain

Nothing has purified me I heard the paralytic
whisper: do not touch me when I die
and behind the golden curtains of morning
the slight cries of the brides between rapacity
and the reception with much flesh: the gospel

For sure there is still a lot to weigh
lion or bouncer with knots in the eyes
and underbrush up the ass you're well disguised
or snowed-in high on the roof with some panhandled light
but the inevitable hurricane of delights the future
is easygoing is ready to explode in your face

Translated by Scott Rollins

moore

it is the earth that drifts and rolls through the people
it is the air that sighs and breathes through the people
the people lie inert as earth
the people stand exalted as air
out of the mother's breast grows the son
out of the father's brow blooms the daughter
wet and dry as rivers and banks their skin
as streets and canals they stare into space
their house is their breath
their gestures are gardens
they shelter
and they are free

it is the earth that drifts and rolls
it is the air that sighs and breathes
through the people

Translated by Peter Nijmeijer

terror

in the end the empty road
the endlessly empty road
the empty stones the thousand and one
white steps the split stones
the very long white empty road
the terribly stony road the very
split stones the endless
quickmarch the glass the stones the white
newly exhumed legs of passers-by
right behind the brushwood
nothing conspicuous behind the hills
deserters are shot down
a general farts
across the road a stinking cloud draws
the corpses lie among the white stones
remarkably well hidden
artistically inlaid among the split stones
each cleft is an astonished eye
and the hundreds the endlessly empty eyes
are nobody's and nobody's
are the rages of violence
sometimes disguised as closed cars
they slowly move along the empty white road
but then it's also certain they will vanish
abruptly into the clear bloodstain static at the horizon

Translated by Peter Nijmeijer

Double Metamorphosis

because the flame of the world disperses
into dry wood clouds full of worms clotted blood
because the water of the world evaporates
into ever sleeping mirrors into nets full of waste
i become a bird ascended from the thirst of stars

because a hand buried the hand of love
in an earth full of eyesore sight and biting tears
because an eye killed the eyes of love
with a shadow shy and cunning behind gleaming doors
i became a star ascended from the thirst of birds

Translated by Peter Nijmeijer

i sing the earth earth

i sing the earth earth:
the earth with her carnivalesque superfloodity
with her breakfasting blossoms sadpleased
bells and egglines in her body there
you see the lady with venturous lips
will kiss you the green greatwise world
will kiss you shuddering

with all my gradual instants
i stifle end and beginning
phallic ah uteral oh
ah & oh
they are my eyes yes and no

what if i cast you silks
through the glass of windows
flowers will greet you and
weeping children like skirts
surround you scream and sway
the shriekling the deafening light
all-deadening light in your wings

Translated by Peter Nijmeijer

the river

out of all its arms the river burns beneath the rocks
and under the little sun over the woods
vomits toward telluric roots towards the cloud-tail
and with dilated muzzle straight through the heaving shards
it swims
with capricious warmth across the world

in darkness near its belly voracious flowers bow
and there is a hole and a pool and the cracking and humming
of a couple of dragons not far away in the evening standing
on a grave an owl staring at transparent gallows while
    coarsely
built rocks surround the melodious abyss there

wet tongues ah ever and always hang against the dismal
    mountains
split tongues toothed tongues inflated
droning tongues and in the valleys in the stone and loam
    cocoons
academically singing men so manfully desperately
singing men and women vaguely draping space

but a viper the fine-veined river flounders on and
gnaws at the weeping flesh of the wind
what is the use of the wailing? snow snows across tremulous
and aged eyes to boot and everything disperses in the night
streaming guilelessly unrestrained though unreleased
from the wailing night

Translated by Peter Nijmeijer

rousseau le douanier

paris is six feet higher than mexico
paris is a gray sail
mexico a motley boat

we go sailing like serpents
the family goes sailing
the mother bears an egg
the father totes a branch

the child stands and is
the staring moon

Translated by Peter Nijmeijer

I Reel a Little Revolution Off

I reel a little revolution off
I reel a lovely little revolution off
I am no longer of land
I am water again
I carry foaming chalices on my head
I carry shooting shadows in my head
A mermaid rests on my back
On my back rests the wind
The wind and the mermaid sing
The foaming chalices ripple
The shooting shadows fall

I reel a lovely little rustling revolution off
And I ripple I fall and I sing

Translated by James S. Holmes

Hans Plomp

◆◆◆

HANS PLOMP was born in Amsterdam, 29 January, 1944. He made his literary debut at the end of the sixties with short stories and novels about the 'hippie' scene in Amsterdam. He characterizes himself as a 'post-beat' writer and has been very active performing his poetry at various local and international festivals. Plomp regularly travels to the Far East (India, Nepal) and his work shows his preoccupation with matriarchal societies and anti-nuke activities.

Poetry:

Gekkenwerk (Madness), 1973
De liefdesoorlog (The Love War), 1979
Venus in Holland, 1981

Novels:

De ondertrouw (The Marriage Banns), 1968
Het Amsterdamse dodenboekje (The Amsterdam Book of the Dead), 1970
Satan ontmaskerd (Satan Unmasked), 1973

Short Story Collections:

De Chinese kruiwagen (The Chinese Wheelbarrow), 1969
Huize de slapeloze nachten (House of the Sleepless Nights), 1971
Brigadier Snuf rookt stuff (Sergeant Snuff Smokes Stuff), 1972
In de buik der moeder natuur (In the Belly of Mother Nature), 1977
Kort geleden (Not Long Ago), 1979
Gedroomde reizen met vrouwen (Dreamed Voyages with Women), 1982

INCUBATE ME, SUCCUBUS

(strictly personal)

Darling,
deep below my will
lurks a monster, out to kill,
out to hurt and out to snare
lovely things still unaware.
Do not touch and do not trust,
it may hurt you just for lust.

Very gently in the day
with the butterflies I play,
but when I'm asleep at night,
here's my monster,
out to fight,
killing
what I kiss by light.

Darling, come into this hell
full of stale and pubic smell.
Darling, penetrate me now,
pierce my heart and tell me how
I can tame my crocodile,
I can make a monster smile.
Incubate me, succubus.

Lady, I don't want no war,
yet my serpent crawls ashore.
Darling, I don't like to kill,
but my jackal wants his fill.

Lover, lick my bloodshot eyes,
change this hell to paradise.
Swallow me and spit me out,
kiss my hairy grisly snout.
Incubate me, succubus.

Snake for snake,
beast for beast.
Push and pull,
mourn and feast.

Even monsters cannot hate
when they're looking for a mate.
Hypnotise me with your hips,
lady, kiss my lying lips.
Do not fear my jealous ape,
hold me, let me not escape.
Incubate me, succubus.

A LADDER TO THE SKY

Paradise is here,
it just needs people
to love it.
The same old wind rustling in the trees,
my moods keep changing forever
inclining to beauty
dear mistress of my fate
still my shadow falls on her so often.

Aye the divine perception
I am ready, let it come to me.
Life at it's fullest
let me live it, let it come to me.
Aye the great worry
may it end,
let the mind play
second fiddle to the heart.

There is laughter and joy at sunrise
always somewhere on this planet:
I have heard it in the Himalayas
and on Crete,
but not in the city
with it's wailing sirens
roaring engines bloody coughs.
Harvarakalla!
Erase it from my memory.

Paradise is here,
this tree waving at itself,
at me,
at anyone who cares and who relates to it,
the passer-by, the bird,
the dog or the suspicion,
all there to take or leave.

A lover of the day and of the night
including both in darkness and in light,
aye let it come through me fully
let me flower to my utmost
into my essential shape
as flowers flower without a trace of doubt
through many transformations
to their exquisite and self-contained reality.

This power love, the one great motivator
generating beauty splendor energy,
the scientist pays no attention to it,
save biologists who call it procreation;
neurologists claim it's a state of madness
that disfigures all perception of reality.
Aye why worry,
they don't know what they're missing.

Out of sheer need
we have become experts on love,
we have mastered the powers of darkness
to work with the powers of light.
There is no light or dark,
there's transmitting and receiving

as death is turned into a ladder to the sky
instead of grub's grub.

Let me flower beyond my self-appointed mission,
let me be in the roots that survive,
let the netherworld manifest freely,
aye let new realities unfold.

THE HEART OF THE DEPRESSION

My doubts turn into debts,
I'm dying.
The low clouds of my memory
rain poison, poison me.
The snake inside me desperately twists,
cobwebs cover my balls,
my love is dead.

I watch myself,
singing out my pain.
My prospects none,
my heaven overcast.
A frozen shadow licks my heart:
my past.
No sun to melt,
no air to fill my wings.
My cold mind stings,
my feelings gone.
Where is my dog?

Come back, lost son,
don't wander blindly
in a land of riches.
Come back, Medusa's daughter,
don't throw the boomerang
of your revenge.

Yes, time is running out
and light is growing weak,
so use it well.
Know your ways in darkness
and know the path through hell.

THE BEAST IS LOOSE!

The Beast is loose! The Beast is loose!
Although I have not seen it yet,
the world around me looks upset.
Everywhere they're running fast,
indeed the bravest are the last,
but everyone is fleeing now:
The Beast is loose, we don't know how.

Parents crying to their gods,
on their knees, pathetic clods.
As the age-old nightmare rides
everybody runs and hides.
The Beast is loose!
Yet the Goddess of the wood
knows and smiles: it feels so good.
The Beast is loose . . .

Everybody seems to know,
no doubt, then, it must be so.
Looks like I'm the only one
who's still happy, having fun.
The only one who did not see.
God, maybe, that Beast is me!

DROP THAT BOMB!

So die world,
drop that bomb and die.
Stop your loathsome threat, you cowards,
drop your bomb and die!
You are much more scared than I,
I don't need bombs to stay free.
I am immortal
I've been through hell
I cried and screamed
I fought and prayed
I died under your tortures.
I died with the corpses I ate
I burned with the trees
I burn to heat my house,
I am the fly I kill
I am death for many creatures
I am death.
So die world,
let your corpse rot in the soil of earth.
I'd rather feel free
among your ruins,
than be a mad prophet
along your highways!
So die now world,
return into the Black Womb
to be born again.

SONG TO OUR ANCESTORS

I eat the creamy yoghurt,
but I never milk the sheep.

A song to mankind,
to the beauty that makes life.
Song to our ancestors,
who found the brilliant way
to get sweet honey from the bee,
soften our beast of prey,
and change grains into bread
by subtle alchemy...
A song to she
who milks the cow
and keeps the fire
and spins the wool
to dress a fool like me.
A song to you,
who found the words and music
for my song.
A song to her,
whose wisdom has delivered me
from killing every creature that I see.

I DON'T WANT NO GURU

Wherever we look, wherever we go,
the holy father leads the show.
Tell us god, or holy son,
where have all the goddesses gone?
Listen, I don't want no guru!
No Jesus, no Mao, no Marx, no Buddha,
no Satan, no Krishna, no Zarathustra!
No leaders down here or up above,
I just want to feel my lady love.

Women of the universe,
only you can end this curse.
Freya, Venus, Nehal, Isis,
will you still allow this?
Do come down and show your face,
bring this stinking world some grace.

We don't need no virgin-mother,
we don't need no tyrant father,
we don't need no murdered son,
we need woman!
We need sweet lady love,
just lady justice,
great lady magic,
to heal the sick.

No Moloch, no Kronos, no Baal, no Allah,
but Shakti, Astarte and sweet Surya,
No gurus or leaders on earth or above,
but you forever, lady love.

Bert Schierbeek

◆◆◆

BERT SCHIERBEEK was born 28 June, 1918 in the small Dutch village of Glanerbrug on the German border. In 1940 he went to study in Amsterdam but German occupation forced him into the Resistance. His experiences of this were chronicled in two conventional novels published immediately after the War. Schierbeek has been active in the annual Poetry International Festival in Rotterdam, has been a Fellow at the University of Iowa's International Writing Program and is now Dutch Writer in Residence at the University of Michigan in Ann Arbor.

Books:

Terreur tegen terreur (Revolt Against the Past), 1945
Gebroken Horizon (Broken Horizon), 1946
Het boek Ik (The Book I), 1951
De andere namen (The Other Names), 1952
Op reis door Spanje (Travels Through Spain), 1952
Op reis door Italië (Travels Through Italy), 1954
De derde persoon (The Third Person), 1955
De gestalte der stem (The Shape of the Voice), 1957
De tuinen van Zen (The Gardens of Zen), 1959
Het kind der tienduizenden (The Child of Thousands), 1959
Het dier heeft een mens getekend (The Animal Has Drawn a Man), 1960
Ezel mijn bewoner (Donkey, My Inhabitant), 1963
Een groot dood dier (A Great Dead Beast), 1963
Een broek voor an octopus (Pants for an Octopus), 1965
Een grote dorst (A Great Thirst), 1968
Inspraak (Speak-In), 1970
De deur (The Door), 1972
In- en uitgang (The Way In & Out), 1975
Vallen en opstaan (Falling & Standing Up), 1977
Weerwerk (Keeping It Up), 1977
Betrekkingen (Relations), 1979
Een tik tegen de lucht (A Tap Against the Air), 1979
Work in progress: *Binnenwerk (Inside Out)*

BINNENWERK *(Inside Out)*

Cross-sections from
A Compositional novel

when
when my father
(he so wanted to reach ninety)
had reachd ninety
he then fell down
that is: he went out
       without a hat under
       the blazing sun walking
       on the lawn
       on his crutches

these crutches he'd had since
his eighty-second year
then he fell because he thought
he'd still be able to jump rope

so then
eight years after that jumping rope
he fell down again
about this he said:
           while I lay there
           I knew: this is the last time
           I'm going to fall
           no, no images from the past
           that comes later on
           I just lay there in the grass
           and I could smell it

and odor of hay
because it was so warm
it also lay a little flat
like I was
I could also see very clearly
the roses, the violets and the
sweet williams in the border
also not so fresh anymore
smell them I could not
their colors I did see
all a little witherd
it was clear
it was summer's last legs
under the sun
I felt no pain
maybe somewhat elated
the gravity perhaps
like this I crawld to the wall
of the ABC (Ancient Boys Center)
I and my crutches weighd nothing
I pulld myself up to the windowsill
of the ABC and thought
it began with this
I taught with them for forty years
and now I'm ending up with them

I zoom away
bizniss class KLM
Chicago—Amsterdam
to get to him
nevertheless
too late

he had
they told me
still said:
(as he was saying goodbye
to his friends—80 of them—
the afternoon before the night
he died)

      if you don't accept
      your getting older that's
      the sign of a badly spent
      life

but death is when
you stop saying anything
and others repeat
what you said
so he also said:

      talking with yourself
      and all those others
      usually makes you lonesome
      everyone says something else
      even when he's saying the same thing
in other words
above Nova Scotia
Octavio Paz said

      a human being is a creature of words
      without them he cannot be graspd
sure:
    it slides by
    very slowly
    towards a light
    of nothing
    someone who goes away
    goes away

someone who stays away
farther and farther away

he liked to be standing in the center
loved a full house
liked to speak with a brittle voice
vulnerably resiliant but unbreakable

you drive by
you see the smoke from the chimney
(the cremetorium)
and you think
there he goes
altho it's not even certain
that it's his smoke
and you see him strolling
one summer morning in his long
underwear through the garden
he spoke with the trees he said
and the birds that he heard
(altho not at all musical)
and he stood still
(singing is the finest
thing there is)
and you see him standing
by the Orinoco River
to music of Villa Lobos
            on islands lonesome
            among twining lianas
            wed to mighty trees

+++

regarding flying, Marcel asks me
well what actually happens
you take off
that goes real fast I guess
says he and his eyes search
an indeterminate spot in the
sky and he raises his
head to that spot

and then you fly he sighs
maybe quite high and well above
the clouds and up there above you it's
all blue and if it's cloudy
below you it's all white
there may well be a landscape

say I there might be some mountains
stacks of mountains and white
wisps that get moved by
the wind like white rivers
not a bird in sight not even
in the blue . . . says Marcel
so you get bored and what do
you do then say I who take off
my shoes ask for a gin-and-tonic
and look at a film
after we've gotten a bite to eat
and the film is calld 'Electric Horseman'
perhaps says Marcel so as to have something
up there to look at after all
say-I yeah and that when you're flying to
New York as we did following the Sun and
are thus flying through time zones and that way

arrive only an hour later than you left
Marcel says but you *are* in flight for seven
hours say-I yes and when the Sun is shining
you can see below you the shadow of the plane
flying over mountains valleys rivers cities
trees towns roads and canals and as you
descend the shadow gets closer and
when you land you land in your own shadow
in short you fly towards the light and
descend into your own shadow
says Marcel considering this so it's
something like dying
Then
you sit and wait
at Kennedy Airport
to fly is to wait
for United Airlines
and read:

      it is the word
      that works
      the verb
      wound . . .

a man shuffles along
hands me a calling card
with his name on it: Eliot Wordsworth
and it read:

      "I am a deaf mute
      I sell ballpoints
      50 cents a piece
      Please buy one.
      Thank you."

I buy one
try it out first
give him a dollar
and write down
with this ballpoint
      was it the word
      workd now
      or the wound
I know
that at night
they both open up
their sourpuss
bats fly
in and out
they hang between yr teeth
the roof's rattling
your head's full of
nestling birds
and incomplete sentences
a stutter
on the threshold
of
      says Octavio Paz
      words do and die
      like people live and die

"It's all America
it's all included Sir"
(as I pay the bill)
"Watch your step
kids
be good
don't talk too much

obey the law
watch out
if you don't
the watchman will
have a good day"

you step in
standing at the entrance
Eliot Wordsworth
gesticulating noisily
      his pens gone
      his money gone
that's how
money gesture and words
pass from hand to hand
a desolate paradise
sweeps around you

++

Dennis Banks is my friend says Spotted Elk
we were not cowards
Indians were never cowards tho at times I was scared
to fly you've got to be a man
you've got to regulate your life and yr children's life
have your money and a job and take care of my three
daughters Faith Hope and Love
haven't seen them in three years
(big tears) I'm tired
(more tears)

you have to understand Indians and make people
understand Indians
I prayd in the church (crosses himself)
I got grade school, high school, got college
sociology got alcoholic
I saw Ira Hayes raise the American flag on Iwo Jima
he became a national hero and got forgotten and died of
drinking—if you don't think about things in time
that is, think beforehand that does happen
(raises his fist) power he yells
I know Dennis Banks, Russell Means, Clyde Bellecourt,
Vernon Bellecourt I drank with Raymond Yellow Thunder
at Pine Ridge Wounded Knee in 1890
it wasn't a battle there
it was mass murder
(starts to sob and sing in Lakota)
I'm not supposed to cry
I've got to be a man
we aren't cowards
(he screams)
look at Manhattan Island Plymouth Rock Wounded Knee
Raymond Yellow Thunder got beaten up
beat up awful bad and died of that
in Gordon Nebraska

       don't come here like that w/ rifles and swords
       to attack us . . .
       what good does it do you people to take w/
       violence what you can easily get
       w/ affection . . .
       or to wipe out those who provide you
       w/ food . . .
       lay down and sleep peacefully w/
       my women and children

laugh and I'll enjoy your company, people
Spotted Elk: Powhatan once said this to Capt. John Smith
Powhatan wasn't a coward
he *thought different*
It's so true what Vallejo wrote:
a human is a sad mammal that combs itself

Translated by Charles McGeehan

Simon Vinkenoog

♦♦♦

SIMON VINKENOOG was born in Amsterdam, 18 July, 1928. He has written on Eastern relgions, hallucinogenic drugs, the occult sciences as well as translating books such as Huxley's *The Doors of Perception* and Artaud's theories on theater. He worked for UNESCO in Paris from 1949-1956, and was an anthologizer of the Dutch experimentalist movement of the 1950s. Vinkenoog regularly mc's poetry events as well as the annual One World Poetry Festival in Amsterdam.

Poetry:

Wondkoorts (Wound Delirium), 1950
Land zonder nacht (Country Without Night), 1952
Heren zeventien (Gentleman Seventeen), 1953
Lessen uit de nieuwe school van taboes (Lessons from the New School of Taboos), 1955
Onder (eigen) dak (At (own) Home), 1957
Spiegelschrift (Mirror Writing), 1962
Eerste gedichten 1949-1964 (First Poems), 1964
Wonder boven wonder (Wonder of Wonders), 1971
Mij best (My Best), 1976
Made in Limburg , 1978
Poolshoogte/Approximations, 1981

Novels:

Zolang te water, 1954
Wij helden (We Heroes), 1957
Hoogseizoen (High Season), 1962
Liefde (Love), 1965
Vogelvrij (Outlawed), 1967
Proeve van communicatie (Experiments in Communication), 1967
Weergaloos (Unequalled), 1968
Leven en dood van Marcel Polak (Life and Death of Marcel Polak), 1969
Het huiswerk van de dichter (The Poet's Homework), 1977
De andere wereld (The Other World), 1978

NEUROBLAST: A BATTLE SONG AND LOVE POEM

for Jef Last, on his 70th birthday,
2nd of May 1968

I

Your heart beats on, amigo
inside out and outside in!

Who is ever going to tell the story
of the tears that were shed on the first row
of the revolution, a free ticket to speed through
the ranks, and the quick looks into the wings?

No heaven above your head, amigo, and
not an inch of terra firma beneath your feet.

Who can stop the word from going its way
to the big the small, the poor the rich,
through the fear and confusion of the times,
to bring on peace, surrender?

Who's going to prevent people from recovering,
rediscovering themselves ever again,
unceasingly, by oneself, in one's own life,
surrounded by friends?

A roaming bird is the poet,
going ever further to get back his breath

ever approaching, closer and closer by,
ever lower his nosedive into the world,
ever higher he spreads his wings,
ever closer approaching his horizons as well,
ever bolder and more courageous his pen,
ever more accurate the firing from his heart,
his eye more generous,
his knowledge law and conscience.

II

He doesn't search and he doesn't find,
your perennial reporter, interpreter, courier,
translator, messenger, decipherer:
he observes and describes—
his pen dipping into the earth's blood, baptized,
his blood curdled by horror,
his handwriting a weapon
his hand guided by experience,
his arsenal the alphabet,
in which the human lies embedded,
biding his time . . .

he chronicles and lays things bare, liberates
in the solitariness of the class conflict,
in the community of perpetuity,
ready ever and again
for fusion and union
yielding and surrender
contact and orgasm,
eros set free—responsibility.

Tribulations jubilations
touching throbbing hearts
the earth a spinning humming top,
centri-fugal and
centri-petal.

To words of water for the fire later,
a bridge between the sky and the earth:

Fellow traveller and contemporary,
ally and cohort, life's artery:
the quotidian word
just as necessary as our daily bread
just as necessary as our recreation

and playing the games of game-playing

III

Who reveals the real?
Who redeems the dream?
Whose weeping, laughing, loving?

Between dawn and dusk
a human being as naked
as his words and deeds,
his trenches and his barricades,
his profits and losses,
his knowledge and his faculties,
his friends and his enemies.

Any man is strong enough
to strike them down:
the borders.

The dangerous borders between people,
the closed doors, the closets and the walls,
the box-offices, sales counters and waiting rooms,
where somebody's still waiting for somebody else,
who's no werewolf,
nor a mere co-worker or collaborator,
but a companion in the game.

IV

It's getting rough in the streets:
clobbering clubs are called 'the brutal truth':
power is manifesting itself everywhere,
making a stand, protesting, being released.

"*Was fällt, das soll man stürzen,
dass es noch schneller falle.*"
"One strikes out at that which is collapsing,
to bring it down all the faster."
(Nietzsche, in Jef Last's *Über die Provokation*)

Revolution is an everyday set of goods
it is a fire behind one's eyes
it is music in your ears
it is the breath that moves you, drives you on,
it is the wind you get caught up in,
it is a permanent confrontation—
a life's work: the artwork Humankind

a masterpiece,
from apprentice to journeyman and master,
and back again: since someone who writes
abides, treads his own path,
goes through and lives by his own 'other way'
all the way
lives all out empty within,
for a printing symbol, a character
that demonstrates, bears witness

The heart keeps on beating
and the wind goes on blowing
into a fire that blazes on undying
—the writer in his 'being human'
greets you with words as sweet
as the glowing sunlight of dawn.

(((((((H O L L A N D I T I S)))))))

Forgotten?
What it was about?
What the matter was?
Do you recall?
In the web of recollection,
the short- and the long-term memory:
an all-out fight, with the weapons of right,
lashing out at murder with the word,
with the dream countering the madness
of the general who says:
"There are more important things than peace"
O yeah? general-diplomat? *What then? Life?*

Is it a fact? is it reality?
Fuck it. Let your imagination speak to you, sport with you,
you're doing your dancing on a volcano,
there are more craven ways to fade away
than in the fighting for your rights,
from embryo to heap of bones,
for your freedom, your free word,
your free thoughts, your free feelings,
let them have their say, please,
your very own inborn potentialities.

THE MIRACLE'S NAME IS PEACE! IT LIVES AND BREATHES!
(never done struggling & ever ready.)

"Nur für Verrückte!" (Only for Madmen!) wrote Hermann Hesse
over the entry to the Magic Theater.

And: "Never will the poet be able to be a leader.
He can just take his readers up to this point,
and then they alone must jump into the abyss."
Hey! caterpillar, snake, butterfly or eagle, hawk,
bully or martyr, have you forgotten how to jump?
Can you still weep, sing, scream, pray, plead, cheer, laugh?
Then laugh, cheer, plead, pray, scream & cry with us:
You don't fight with the weapons of your opponent,
You don't fight with the lies and the fear,
you don't fight with programs and guidelines,
you don't fight with systems and prescriptions,
rules and strategies, no, you don't fight against
the nervewracking apparatus
that's gone haywire, utter violence run wild,
pursued by the anguish of not knowing anymore,
owing to the—do you remember?—forgetting,
the super-soothing, very simple
pure and sure knowledge
that the point in question is Peace.
Which transcends your reasoning.

There's plenty of distraction on the way of the heart: what
with feuding, wrangling, snags, misunderstandings,
quarrels, strife, arguments, tiffs,
—conflicts, grudges, revenge, contradictions.

Let it all go, folks, let all the envy and enmity
go by—so precious your time . . .

And aah, Haig, man,
what do you know of
colors, aromas and fragrance,
the great leap forward in the freefalling void:

your personal confrontation, readiness,
solidarity.

Little man a bit, a piece, a corpuscle of humanity.
The voice of the people. Poetry.
At times it's a hit: You go
OFF   to here and now: Peace.
Quiet, stillness and—a moment—of attention.
As if your whole life were waiting
between the lines
of dying and being born.

The poet takes you a *long way.*
He can bring it real close to home for you.
From nowhere anymore and heading for nowhere,
or wherever from, and up to now.
Everything different, he says. At times reprogramming is
waiting for you, your high & highly personal
stock quotation, currencies, bonds, and
a handshake, or a smile.
War can commence in the home.
Peace can prevail at the kitchen table.
War can pitch camp in your bed.
Peace can live in your words and deeds.

It isn't a question of your dreams, your thoughts,
your ideas, your illusions; nor of your truth—
which is *not* only yours.

In what stands written here because it's true,
your life is mirrored, forcing,
thru affliction and labor pains,

the delivery from fear,
the running prologue to the first free, enlightened
breathing with relief.

Yes, because it's true. For all we've got's in common.
For we've got to share in pleasures & burdens,
not to force people or to manipulate them.
For the first articulation, for the first intention
to serve good will.

For the world of goodwill. The reservoir of love,
the arsenal of light.
the cosmic planetary ecological
common sense.
Sun on the horizon.
Children playing.
And we 'grownups' in such a dangerous game.
Think of it. I, for one, can't answer little
Anna asking: "Why do they make that—war?"

Not a minute to lose.
All the time in the world.
Struggle everywhere.

Ah! Aha! the young laugh
the first day
the last flag
beginning without
end

Halfway there *hollanditis* and eternal yearning:
reconnoitering, stalking, tracking down
these *are* tactics and strategies

not just improvisations and situations
accidents, coincidences,
but making certain and deciding

BAN WAR FROM THE WORLD!
Starting with Holland—Now!
It's FORBIDDEN to FORBID

*(For One World Poetry's "War On War" at
Melkweg & Paradiso, Amsterdam; 2-11 Oct. '81)*

These poems translated by Charles McGeehan

Anton Constandse

♦♦♦

ANTON CONSTANDSE is in his eighties and the father of the humanist movement in the Netherlands. He is an anarchist as well, having written important works on Bakunin, Erasmus, freedom, and international politics. His principal publisher is Meulenhoff (Amsterdam).

HOLLANDITIS

An Address given by Anton Constandse at the One World Poetry Festival, Paradiso Hall, Amsterdam, October 7, 1981

Dear Friends,

The man standing before you here suffers from a serious contagious disease. The facial color coming with it is generally red, sometimes pink, but today we find also Christian shades among them, and some yellow, lilac and even black. The epidemic is spreading everywhere, and it is called *hollanditis*. Actually we're dealing with a psychic aberration, and it is not impossible we'll be put in quarantine presently, isolated from the healthy Europeans, who are in danger of being contaminated by us. For what is *hollanditis*? It is the belief that nuclear arms are leading us to the abyss, that stationing the newest American missiles increases the possibility we will be part of the future battlefield and will be killed *en masse*.

Where, however, would those missiles have to go, if all other nations had similar opinions? In Western Germany, colonies of hollanditis have already been discovered. Two hundred thousand select American troops are stationed there, with hundreds of subterranean stocks of the most recent nuclear arms, more than in America itself. But greater and greater masses of Germans are taking to the streets to protest. Everywhere we see the slogan "Yankee Go Home"; President Reagan is pictured as a wild cowboy, and two thirds of the Western Germans reject the placement of new American nuclear arms on German territory. All this was done by the Dutch. Their hollanditis threatens to infect all of Western Europe.

What has caused the growing fear of the total destruction of battlefield Europe? A memorandum of August 8, 1980, was signed by President Carter, the peanut-grower who went on the road as an evangelist and reserved a place for each of us in heaven. The note was based on the idea that a "restricted nuclear war" has become possible now. What does "restricted" mean? War in Europe and, from this position, the destruction of the whole Russian military potential in one blow. Those Russians could hit back a little, mainly in Europe, but they would not be able to do much against America. Or what is much? When the American defense minister left office on January 20, 1981, he estimated his country could get away with twenty-two million dead, one tenth of the population. Whereas European Russia as a nation would have ceased to exist.

What was new about this theory? Well, until then NATO had always claimed nuclear bombs would never be used, but served only to deter, and to maintain the military balance. That was a strange enough thought. For the sake of that balance it had to be hoped the Russians would arm themselves madly, to scare the Americans. They have always trailed behind. The Americans were the first to develop the atomic bomb, the H-bomb, long distance bombers, nuclear submarines, rockets with more than one nuclear head, cruise missiles and neutron bombs. To maintain the balance of terror it was crucial that the Russians take part in this race. But with that memorandum, a new road was taken: a nuclear war would be possible and necessary. The weapons were there to be used. According to the most reliable Sipri Report, 43% of international armament is financed by NATO countries, 26% by the Warsaw Pact. There are now 60,000 nuclear weapons in the world, 30,000 of which are in American and 20,000 in Russian hands; the rest in China, England, France, India, and even South Africa and Israel. The total overkill is awesome. These arms could easily kill a hundred billion people, twenty-five times the world population. Every ministry of defense should rightly be named Ministry of Genocide now.

To protest against this, to reject all this, is now labeled *hollanditis*, as if it were a dangerous disease. This reminds me how Multatuli was called a neurotic in the last century, and someone remarked this neurotic did more for the four million Dutch of his time than all the so-called normal Christians. And now again the true psychopaths are the military leaders and the hysterial cold war propagators, who want to drive us mad with fear of the Russians. But the Russians are almost collapsing under the strain of the arms race. If they would occupy Western Europe with its enormous industries but lack of raw materials, they would have to deal with a resistance of many times more people than there are in Poland. They would survive that neither economically nor politically. Yet we have to be kept living in fear of war with them, even though war now means self-destruction. What kind of insane world is this? Are we ruled by criminals?

In world literature there is a dreadful projection of the imagination. It is from *The Songs of Maldoror*—the terrible image of a sadistic supreme god: "Sometimes he cried out: 'I have created you, so I have the right to do with you as I please. You have not done me wrong, this I won't deny. I make you suffer because it pleases me.' And he went on with his cruel meal, moving his lower jaw, while his beard full of human blood moved with it."

Have not the theologists often spoken about war as a melting pot, a process of purification, a punishment of God? Yet Bakunin justly remarked: "If a God existed, we would have to abolish him." For the sake of our freedom and our humanity. And thus the human race will have to do away with militarism, before we are destroyed by it. Of course our power is restricted in a small country that has become a protectorate of a world-power. But we have our infectious disease hollanditis with which to resist this useless perishing. What an honor for the majority of the Dutch people! Indeed this majority is aware of the roots of our culture. We find them in the works of Erasmus, apostle of peace in an age of dreadful wars: "Since Christ ordered us to drop our swords, all battle is forbidden, except the most beautiful one—the battle against the true enemies of our faith: greed, anger, ambition and killing. Truly, is there a more unworthy sort of slavery, than being a soldier? And, once the sad sign is given, they become tools of death, either by killing others in horrible ways, or by being killed. They go through so much misery, to get to the most miserable place of all. They submit themselves to so much torture, only to torture others."

The sufferers from hollanditis remember the philosopher Spinoza, certainly no anarchist but a democrat who demanded that the government respect the dignity of the people: "The state may not turn its citizens from reasonable beings into puppets." We think of the former vicar, Bart de Ligt, who was jailed in 1921 because he told people to object against war-service after the terrible onslaught of 1914-1918 "in the name of Jesus Christ, in the name of Karl Marx, of Bakunin (hero, poet of freedom, passionate fighter against all official authority), in the name of Kropotkin with his ethics of mutual aid."

In the war year 1914, professor Leo Polak, one of our greatest humanists, opened his lectures in Amsterdam with a refutation of war philosophy. He said: "International and united is the objective spirit. This will kill war." The Nazis killed him in a concentration camp. He ended his lecture with the prophet Micah's dream of the great Liberator who would come to unite all nations. Polak knew however, as a philosophical free-thinker, that no redeemer would come and that people would have to liberate themselves and each other from destruction and fear of death.

From Erasmus to our present pacifists, Dutch culture has been shaped and ennobled by enemies of war and friends of peace. For *this* Holland we want to live.

Translated by Hans Plomp

POCKET POETS SERIES